THREE KEYS
TO BECOMING A
RESPONSIBLE
STUDENT

*How to be a Successful Student
in Middle and High School*

CURT THOMAS

ISBN: 0615984177
ISBN 13: 9780615984179
Library of Congress Control Number: 2014904678
Curt Thomas Unlimited, LLC, Orangeburg, SC

CONTENTS

DEDICATION

This book is dedicated to my three wonderful sons:
Tyler Michael Thomas, Preston Kyle Thomas,
and Michael Daniel Thomas.
To them I owe my life and dedication to being a better
Father

INTRODUCTION

G reetings. My name is Curt Thomas, and you are currently reading the book entitled *Three Keys to Becoming a Responsible Student.* This book is designed for the student in middle through high school. I believe that if you are reading this book, you are part of the brightest, most intelligent, and smartest group of young men and women on the face of planet. I believe you have something special within you, and this book is designed to help you discover your greatness. It is designed to help you become more responsible. No doubt this is a pivotal time in your life. There is a worldwide call for students, like you, who are in these grades to become more responsible. Attention has been widely focused on the irresponsibleness of students in middle and high school.

However, a few of us adults realize there is "nothing new under the sun," meaning we have done some of the same things and made the same mistakes as you may have. Some of us got caught stealing, made wrong decisions, and grew up less fortunate. Many of us had everything we needed to stay out of trouble. Some of us lived in the suburbs and were from wealthy homes, but still found trouble. Irresponsibleness has no favorite race, color, religion, or culture. We are all products of our decisions. The good news is that if you're alive and reading this book, you have a chance to change your life's direction. You have the gift of choice. You have the universal right to alter your route to failure, and get back on the road to a better life. Remember, you can learn from someone who has "been there and done that." The wisest of people know that learning and listening to their elders' advice is the key to avoiding and overcoming life's failures. If we made it, so can you.

Before getting started reading this book, do me a favor. It's very important that you do this. Find your mother, and give her the biggest hug you can. She may currently be at work, but as soon as she gets home, I want you to grab her and squeeze her real tight, and tell her, "Thank you." She's probably going to look at you strange and figure you've done something wrong, but say, "Mom, everything is OK. I just want to thank you."

Why? Why do I want you to do that? I am the father of three wonderful boys (Tyler, Preston, and Michael), and I know I played an important role in their lives, but their mother plays a *spectacular* role! I feel like Abraham Lincoln, who said, "All that I am and all that I hope to be, I owe it to my mother." The same could be said of my father. I love that quote because, like Les Brown (world renown motivational speaker), my mother does not have a degree or any formal education from a college or university. However, she does have a PhD in *motherhood!* She raised my brother, Bernard, and I the best she could, and I love her very much. We were not wealthy, but my mother and father did their best to ensure we had a chance at life. They instilled love and a sense of responsibility in us. Understanding responsibility is necessary for your success in middle and high school. I will share with you how to do that.

TODAY

I

CHOOSE

Turn the page and continue…

TO BE
RESPONSIBLE!

Note: *Please remember that making responsible decisions* now *will help you toward your* future *goal (to be a teacher, nurse, military member, police officer, fire fighter, model, fashion designer, entrepreneur, etc.)*

CHAPTER 1

WHY IS RESPONSIBILITY IMPORTANT?

The word *responsibility*, in and of itself, hands down, bar none, is the most important word you should keep near your heart—beside the word *respect*. You may already know what you want to be when you grow up. You may want to go to law school or into the medical profession. You may want to enter the military or be a mechanic. Maybe you want to own your own business as an entrepreneur, which I highly recommend. However, before you can do any of those things, you have to understand and harness the word *responsibility*. I will give you *three keys* I've formulated to become a responsible student. If you keep these three keys as a guide, they will take you from middle school to high school—and from high school to college or the military. They will take you to your dreams, but you must keep them close to your heart.

These three keys helped me while I was in middle school. They helped me through high school and in college. They helped me while I served in the United States Air Force. These three keys helped me go from being the lowest person in my high school, college, military, or my job with the highway patrol, to being number one in every occupation I have ever worked. I want to share these keys with you, and if you take them to heart and be more responsible, they will help you reach your dreams. Are you ready?

I will share with you a time in my life when I was irresponsible. When I left middle school and started high school, I was labeled a failure. I will share with you what I did to get back on track with my life.

TODAY

I

CHOOSE

TO BE RESPONSIBLE!

CHAPTER 2

PLAYING TOO MUCH WILL CATCH UP WITH YOU

The first key to becoming a responsible student is **remember**. I want you to remember *why* you need to be responsible.

There is nothing like passing a grade. I remember going from the eighth to ninth grade. I had a great time in middle school. Finally, I was going into the ninth grade. Oh, I was labeled a *freshman* (laughs). You know how it is when you go from one grade to the next. You feel like you are all that and a bag of potato chips (laughs). I remembered going to high school and saying to myself, "I am going to have such a great time. I'm going to play every sport. I'm going to play basketball, and, if I can, I'm going to play football." (I was only five foot five and 110 pounds). I knew I would have a great time.

I remembered going to school on the first day of the new school year and meeting all the guys in my homeroom class. I loved to talk in school! I came home from school each day and went straight to my room to play my game set. Back in the day, I had a Nintendo game console. You probably don't know what that is, do you? Not a Nintendo Wii, but a regular Nintendo with only two buttons. Yes, that was a long time ago (laughs). I would play my Nintendo from the time I came home until it was time to go to sleep, every day. Every day my mother came home from work and said, "Curt…" (me)

"Yes, ma'am, Mama."

"You finished your homework for today?"

"Yes, ma'am, Mama…I did it at school. I'm good…everything is good to go."

She said, "All right. Make sure you do your homework. I don't want you to mess up in school."

I said, "Ahhh man, Mama, I got it. I am good to go."

She asked me and sometimes checked to make sure I was on top of my game, because education was important to my mother and father. They worked hard, and each day they went to work and trusted that I would be responsible enough to go to school. Being the elder of two boys, they expected me to study my lessons, learn them, come home, do my homework, and prepare myself for the next day.

Note: *What are your current distractions? How do you use your time immediately after school? Can you find extra time to study? It will give you a huge advantage when it gets closer to the end of the school year.*

However, let me explain what I did in high school. Every day when I got to school, I didn't pay attention. I didn't even do my homework; as a matter of fact, all I did was play in the ninth grade. I played so much that school felt like a social hang-out. I played around from August to December, and then from December to May. After school I jumped on the game console each and every day. If I didn't play the game, I went down the street to my friend's house to play basketball because, oh, I had *game!* I could play basketball; I could shoot that rock! I had the best jump shot on the block. I was good at basketball and foot-ball. I was the best wide receiver in my neighborhood. I hit all the homeruns when playing baseball. I was the neighborhood athlete. You couldn't tell me anything (laughs). I was also intro-duced to alcohol and marijuana. I tried it once and immediately realized that it was not for me. I decided to stick with being a neighborhood athlete.

The funny thing was that around May, I got nervous because report cards were about to be issued, and all that playing came to mind. When I got my report card, I looked down it and saw an A in English. I was like, "Oh yeah, ain't nothing like having an A, baby!" Another A in physical education too? "Oh yeah, oh yeah, I'm good to go…I'm rocking and rolling," I said to myself. Got to math, and there was an F there, an F for failure. I remembered looking at the

F and saying to myself, "How did that happen? Oh well, it'll be all right." I tried to play it off, but then I read the note at the bottom of the report card: "Student cannot proceed to tenth grade."

TODAY I CHOOSE

Turn the page and continue…

TO BE RESPONSIBLE!

CHAPTER 3

THE PRICE OF IRRESPONSIBILITY

All of a sudden, it wasn't funny anymore. The other kids were excited and were celebrating because they were about to be *sophomores*...but not me, and the reality began to sink in. Wow, I really failed the ninth grade. All I could think about was how I would tell Mama. How would I explain to my mother and father that I didn't pass? All that time, she thought I been studying and maintaining an A average, I was doing the opposite. I had lied. I was irresponsible. It wasn't funny anymore.

I walked to school instead of riding the bus. That day when I walked back home with two of my friends, they laughed and joked about school. One of my buddies said, "Curt, what's wrong?"

I replied, "Nothing...I'm good; I'm good, not feeling too well." These guys were excited to be moving up a grade, and they didn't know I failed. I had never failed before in my life!

When I got home, I didn't want to play the Nintendo game. As a matter of fact, I didn't even turn on the television set. I heard the car pull into the driveway when Mom and Dad came home. Then both car doors slammed shut as they exited. My brother sat in the living room and I sat at the kitchen table. I was so nervous. I couldn't think straight and didn't know what I should do or say. How would I tell my mother that I failed? How would I tell my father I didn't pass?

I saw a Bible on the table, so I opened it and *pretended* I was reading as my mother and father came through the door. *It's amazing how religious you get when you think you're going to get a butt cutting (laughs).*

My brother ran to her and said, "Hey, Mama, I got my report card. I passed. Mama, I passed."

She was so happy and excited for him. She gave him a kiss and a huge hug, and so did my dad. Then she looked at me and said, "Hey Curt, is everything all right?"

I said, "Yeah, Mama, everything is all right. Just reading my Bible...reading Psalms 23."

Then she asked, "You got your report card today, didn't you?"

I said, "Yes, Mama, I did. I have it right here."

She said, "Well...congratulations then, right?"

Then I said, "Well, Mom, I have something to tell you, I passed English, P.E., and I got good grades. I did real good...but one class I didn't do too well in, and it's math."

At the time, my mom didn't know the ins and outs that if I didn't pass math, I wasn't going to the next grade. So she said, "That's OK, just do better next year."

I replied, "No, Mama, let me show you my grades."

"Let me take a look at it," she said.

I said, "You're going to be mad at me. I didn't pass the ninth grade and I'm sorry, Mama...Mama, I'm so sorry." As I said this, tears flowed from my eyes.

For the first time in my life, my mother started crying, and it was because I had hurt her. I really hurt her that time. Tears flowed down her face and her bottom lip trembled. All that time, she had *trusted* me to be responsible, to go to school, to get good grades so I could graduate. She trusted me to do my homework, and I didn't do it. I let her down for the first time. I looked at her and saw how much I hurt her because I lied to her. She cried, followed by constant sniffles. My mother looked at me and said, "Curt, how could you do this to me? I work too hard every day for you boys to go to school and not play. How could-you-do-this-to-me?" My mom went into her bedroom, still crying.

At this time, I caught the eyes of my father, who was a preacher, and he was so angry. All he said was, "You made your mama cry... you made your mama cry." He went into the bedroom to console her.

My brother, Bernard, was somewhere in the corner of the living room, looking on with excited eyes. He knew his older brother was about to get a whooping, and he wasn't about to miss this awesome action! (laughs.)

So here I was, walking to my room, and I could still hear the sniffles of my mom's crying down the hallway. I began to cry myself because I didn't want to let my mother down. I don't care who you are. I don't care how big and bad you are, or how bad you think you are, *you don't ever want to make your mother cry.* Not the one who brought you into this world. It does something to you. It eats your soul to hear your mother cry. So, that night I went to bed and vowed that I would never let my mother down again. Not like that. I remember the look on my mother's face as she began to cry. It was because of *me!* That thought and the image of her crying stayed with me. That night I remembered why: why I was supposed to go to school, and why I was supposed to do my homework. I wasn't going to do play around again.

So all summer I played it off, and a week before school, my homeboys came over and said, "Hey, Curt, how does it feel to be going to the tenth grade?"

I replied, "Man, what happened was…man, that teacher don't like me, man! She failed me. She failed me, dawg."

They said, "What?"

I said, "Yeah man, she don't like me, but I'm going to do what I gotta do. I'll be all right." There I was, trying to act hard in front of my boys.

A lot of us like to use that excuse, that a certain teacher doesn't like us because we failed or didn't make good grades. Let me tell you a secret. Even if your teacher does not like you, if you are doing what you are supposed to do—studying, passing your tests—your teacher, by law, has to pass you. Saying that your teacher "does not like you" is no excuse for failure. I came to grips with that.

Note: If you fail, *don't blame your teacher! It's not the teacher's fault… it's yours! Admit it and do better.*

So when the next school year started, I had the complete em-barrassment of seeing my classmates go to their tenth grade home-room classes while I sat in the ninth grade homeroom *again*. All the new ninth graders, who had just left middle school, walked in the room and looked at me, like, "We don't know this fool. He must've failed last year."

I had to deal with the embarrassment of being in the ninth grade again. Who could I talk to now? Who could I flirt with now? The answer was no one, because I didn't know anyone, plus they only saw me as a failure. I failed because I was irresponsible and because I played around.

TODAY
I
CHOOSE

Turn the page and continue…

TO BE RESPONSIBLE!

Note: Please remember that making responsible decisions now will help you toward your future goal (to be a teacher, nurse, military member, police officer, fire fighter, model, fashion designer, entrepreneur, etc.)

CHAPTER 4

LET RESPONSIBILITY BE YOUR DRIVING FORCE

L et me tell you what I did. I began to take on the responsibility of each subject in high school. I remembered the look on my mother's face from day one of that school year. I said, "You know what? I got to make this happen!" I went on and passed every subject. When it came to math that year, and for the next two years, I passed. My average was so high; I was exempt from those exams. In my day, if you had a high average in a class, you didn't have to take the final exam because your average showed you knew the material. If you made all As, you were exempt from taking final exams. That year, I passed and was able to catch up with my guys, my fellow students, my classmates in eleventh grade. I passed with an A in math. I remembered why.

So if you're in middle school or high school, it's important for you to remember why you are where you are. You have to remember. Have some image or something in your heart that will keep you from going astray. That will keep you on the right path. Let it be your *driving force.* Your reason may be different from mine, but it's your responsibility to remember why. I told you that you have greatness within you. Winston Churchill said, *"The price of greatness is responsibility."*

Note: List three reasons why being responsible should be important to you!

I want you to grab a sheet of paper and a pencil or pen and write down three reasons why you should continue to stay focused in high school or in middle school. Write down three reasons you should take responsibility for your academics and your welfare. My three reasons were (1) My mother. I remembered seeing her crying. I didn't want to see that again. I didn't want to disappoint her ever again, especially knowing I could have done better the first time. I could have been better and been more responsible. (2) I didn't want to let myself down. I knew I was smarter than my behavior. Others looked at me like I was a failure in the ninth grade, and I did not want to be another failure. (3) I wanted to prove to myself and to them that I was smarter than what my behavior showed that first year in the ninth grade.

Write down the three reasons why that you need to remember. Every day, *every* day, look at those three reasons, and remind yourself why you need to be responsible. Put the list in your notebook, in your wallet, in a book bag, in a book, or somewhere you can see it every day. It will help you as you go through your day-to-day activities.

List three reasons why being responsible should be *important* to *you*!

These are the three reasons you should keep near your heart. For example: *I don't want to disappoint my parents* or *I promised my grandmother I would stay out of trouble and make her proud* or *I know I can do better in school then what I am now doing.*—These are just examples to help you with your list of reasons.

1.

2.

3.

I want you to understand something. You will be tempted and tried in ways you never thought of before. You need to look at those reasons daily. Remember those three reasons that you wrote down. Keep the list by you during those "valley time" experiences; it will be your sword and shield to help you make it through. Keep the reasons in front of you, even while you are making mistakes, and you will bounce back. You are going to make mistakes, but if you can remember why, which is my first key; this will help you reach your goal. So that completes my first key, which is the word *remember*. Remember *why* you should be responsible in middle school and in high school.

TODAY

I

CHOOSE

Turn the page and continue…

TO BE RESPONSIBLE!

Note: Please remember that making responsible decisions now will help you toward your future goal (to be a teacher, nurse, military member, police officer, fire fighter, model, fashion designer, entrepreneur, etc.)

CHAPTER 5

IT'S ABOUT YOU

This leads me into my second key, which is **reputation**. The word *reputation*, in simpler terms, is a word that is a reflection of *you*. The word *reputation* is a reflection of *your* personality, the way *you* communicate to people, and *your* history. Can people trust *you*? Can people count on *you* to be responsible? That is *your* reputation. How you get along with people. That is how people view you and remember you.

When I was in the ninth grade, as soon as I became a freshman from middle school, I had the reputation of being "Curt the Flirt" (laughs). When I got in class, I had the reputation of being someone who played around and didn't listen to the teacher. While the teacher was talking, I was talking. I was busy trying to get phone numbers from girls because I was trying to *prove* something to people. I was trying to prove to people that Curt was cool, Curt was "down," Curt was not scared to do anything. I had that reputation and I wanted to live up to it. I figured that if I lived up to my name, everyone would think I was cool. The crazy thing was I really wanted that. What I didn't realize was that trying to live up to my reputation caused me to fail. That reputation of "Curt the Flirt" distracted me from learning my lessons.

Having the reputation of a failure was not fun. Having the reputation as a flirt *is* better than having the reputation of a failure. But having the reputation of being a person who can flirt, talk, laugh, and play sports, but who doesn't have good academics is *not* cool. You don't want that kind of reputation. If you want to have a good reputation, strive to have the reputation of a student people can count on, that people can say, "You know what, that student is going somewhere."

Even in middle school, you can develop the reputation of being a student who goes to class. In high school, you can develop the reputation of completing your assignments on time. Having a good reputation will help you while you're in school. When you have a good reputation as the type of student who always gets the job done, if you don't complete your assignment on time, your teacher will hopefully say, "Wait a minute, wait a minute. Something's wrong. If Keisha didn't pass this test or do her homework, then something's wrong. If Craig didn't turn in his homework, then something is wrong. Let me call his parents and make sure everything is all right. This is not like Keisha, or this is not like Craig, to not do the work." You want to develop that type of reputation, that people can count on you to be responsible.

<u>*Note:*</u> *Write down your top five friends that you hang out with regularly*

If you're taking notes, don't just write down the word *reputation* as it relates to being more responsible in middle school and high school. It's also important that you understand that it is not only you who develops your reputation (I learned this while in the ninth grade), but the crowd and the friends you choose develop it too. They can also label you in a way you did not mean to be labeled. Just because in *your* mind *you're* responsible, when you hang around people who are irresponsible, you will be *labeled* irresponsible. People who are labeled as troublemakers, unreliable, or not responsible will rub off on you. You will be labeled with that same reputation. I don't know why it is like that, but that is just the way it is.

List your top five friends

Note: List the five friends you hang out with the most. This should be a list of friends you talk (connect) or text with the most when in class, during recess, (including by cell phone, Facebook, Instagram, Twitter, etc.), or who live in your neighborhood.

1.

2.

3.

4.

5.

Now that you have your list of your five top friends, write their names down again. Beside their names, write *positive* reasons to keep them as friends and, under that, write the *negative* consequences (what could eventually happen if you stay friends with them).

For an example of *positive* reasons: "Hanging out with Chris will help me stay on the honor roll because he takes his studying seriously." "Texting Samantha often motivates me to try harder in chemistry." "James really hates cigarettes and crime, so I know he will help me stay away from those kinds of peer pressure."

Negative consequences: "Emily is always talking back to the teacher and getting suspended." "Tracey sometimes skips class and sneaks into clubs and lies to her parents." "Mike never turns in his homework and he steals all the time." "Jake bullies other kids." "Diana uses drugs and wants me to try them too."

Write down their names, and ask yourself what will eventually happen to *you* if you continue to hang around these people.

1.

2.

3.

4.

5.

Dr. Steve Maraboli (bestselling author) says, "If you hang out with chickens, you're going to cluck. If you hang out with eagles, you're going to fly." Think about that. "If you hang out with chickens, you're going to cluck, and if you hang out with eagles, you're going to fly." I want you to look at your list of your *top* five friends. Are they helping your reputation while you're in middle school? Are they helping you become more responsible while you're in high school? Think about that—be honest with yourself.

As it relates to you being a more responsible student in middle school and in high school, go back and look at those five names you wrote down. Come to grips with yourself, and ask this important question: What are these relationships doing to me? Are they really helping me, or are they tearing me down? You can't be a *responsible* person *and* hang around with those who are *irresponsible.* That's like a positive and a negative charge, and one will outdo the other. Understand that positive people and people with good reputations have to be around those with similar reputations.

If you want to be successful, if you really want to be successful, you have to make it a *choice* to be responsible. You have to set standards for yourself. It is necessary for you to be more responsible while in middle school and in high school because, after all, you're the *only* person who knows what you want to be when you grow up. You're the only person who knows your dreams. You're not going to reach those dreams until you come to grips with responsibility. All the great ones have done it. You *can* do it too. I'm so glad you're reading this now at this stage in your life.

It is important that you understand that you need to *remember* why you should be responsible. Have those three reasons why you should be responsible. The next key is to understand your *reputation*. Your reputation is all you have to identify yourself in this world. Your reputation is a reflection of you. It tells people who you are, even when people haven't seen you in person. Your name is your reputation. Your reputation can make *or* break you.

Note: Hold yourself to high standards. Don't allow someone else's reputation to contaminate yours.

After I failed the ninth grade, I decided to get better friends. I decided that I would no longer be "Curt the Flirt" but "Intelligent Curt the Flirt" (laughs). I made the decision to be more responsible and to remember what I was supposed to accomplish while in school. I remembered why I attended school.

I passed the ninth grade. I got better friends, and I got better altogether. This leads me to my next key, the last key in becoming more responsible in middle school or in high school.

TODAY

I

CHOOSE

Turn the page and continue…

TO BE RESPONSIBLE!

NOTE: Please remember that making responsible decisions now will help you toward your future goal (to be a teacher, nurse, military member, police officer, fire fighter, model, fashion designer, entrepreneur, etc.)

CHAPTER 6

FOCUS ON WHAT YOU WANT

The last key is **results.** You need to understand, and decide to focus on, results. The word *result* is the least difficult of the three keys. I chose to put it at the end because the word *result* is a derivative of the first two keys. In order to be a more responsible middle school and high school student, you must learn how results can work for you. If you remember why you're in school, remember the reason why you're there, and understand the importance or your reputation; You will get results.

The idea is that you must complete your assignments. You must learn and use the brain that the infinite intelligence has given to you. You can do this if you remember why it is important to you. Remember that you should listen to your teachers because they are the instructors and are teaching you things you don't know. If you remember that truth and keep it close to your heart, you will understand that your reputation is all you have. You will understand that you should cherish it like it's a diamond, because it is a reflection of you. If you keep these keys in your heart and mind, you will get the last key, which will make you so successful. It will help you become more responsible. You will get that last key, which are results.

Lionel Suggs (author) said, "I don't create miracles, I create results." Simply put, if you do the things you're supposed to do and follow those first two keys, the last key, *results,* will come. What do you mean by that, Curt Thomas? Those results will come?

If you are responsible, and you remember why and develop a good reputation, the result will be that you'll go from the sixth grade to the seventh. Next, the seventh grade to the eighth, from a freshman to a sophomore, and then, from a sophomore to a junior, and from a junior to a senior. Finally, from a senior to graduation! We all strive toward the end result, which is graduation.

I heard another speaker say, "We are the sum total of the decisions that we have made." The last key is results. If you focus on the results, you will make it. People will say, "I knew from middle school that he was going to be somebody! It does not surprise me that he is as successful as he is today." "It does not shock me that she has won those many awards; it does not shock me that she was accepted into so many universities." "She proved to me that she was responsible." "In middle school and all throughout high school, he was responsible."

You will make mistakes, but you have to own up to your mistakes. You have another chance to become responsible. You may have gotten caught doing wrong. I have many times. Nevertheless, I owned up to my mistakes. I became responsible, and the results are that I'm progressing. I've won many awards, but I'm still progressing. I've traveled the world, but I'm still progressing. I've shot commercials and met awesome people, but I am still progressing.

<u>Note:</u> *Focus on the things you want in life, not on the things you don't want*

TODAY

I

CHOOSE

TO BE
RESPONSIBLE!

NOTE: *Please remember that making responsible decisions* now *will help you toward your* future *goal (to be a teacher, nurse, military member, police officer, fire fighter, model, fashion designer, entrepreneur, etc.)*

CHAPTER 7

COMMIT TO BECOMING RESPONSIBLE

So there you have it. Those are the three keys that will help you become more responsible in middle school. The three keys are: (1) remember (2) reputation (3) results. They will help you while in high school. Not everybody will do it. Not everybody *wants* to be responsible. I believe that if you're reading this book, you have already made up your mind that you will be responsible. If you make mistakes, it's fine. We all make mistakes. The best part of life is that if you take responsibility for any mistakes, you can still be successful.

I had to learn the hard way, by failing the ninth grade and facing the embarrassment of being viewed as a failure. You know what? That taught me a valuable lesson, and it continues to teach me a lesson today. If I did it once, I can do it again, and so can you.

The *world* is waiting on you now. The world is waiting to see if you'll be responsible or if you will become a statistic. Will you be responsible enough to do your homework and complete your assignments on time? Will you listen to your teacher, be on time for school, be early to class, and graduate? Will you be the one teachers can count on to be responsible and have a great reputation? Will they look forward to you graduating middle school and high school? Are you up to the challenge? If you are, this beautiful world is awaiting you with open arms. It wants to see you achieve your dreams. *I* want to see you achieve your dreams.

Please, keep the word *responsibility* close to your heart. It may help you start your own business one day. Learning to be responsible now may help you get into the college you've dreamed of for years. Making the choice to become more responsible now may save your life tomorrow. If you do this, it will take you places that money and fame won't take you.

TODAY

I

CHOOSE

TO BE RESPONSIBLE!

Contact Information:

Mailing Address: Curt Thomas Unlimited, LLC

803.290.9237

P.O. Box 684

Orangeburg, SC 29116

Email: CurtThomasSpeaks@gmail.com

Facebook: **Curt Thomas Motivational Speaker**

Instagram: **@CurtThomasSpeaks**

Twitter: **@CurtSpeaks**

Made in the USA
San Bernardino, CA
15 April 2017